SUCH LUCK

SUCH LUCK

Sara Backer

FLOWSTONE PRESS

First Flowstone Press Edition • 28 September 2019 、
ISBN 978-1-945824-33-3

In memory of my father,
William R. Backer

LUCK

SUCH

LUCK

Now's the Time

Long ago on the edge of Vienna and lost,
I walk off the map into an alley of street vendors
squatting on tablecloths beside strange treasure:

ebony snakes carved as bracelets, silver coins strung
as necklaces, lace scarves, intricately
painted eggs, tiny porcelain elephants.

I want
everything. I can't
choose.

Someone whistles sharply:
a six-note riff I recognize
from Charlie Parker's saxophone.

Vendors roll tablecloths into sacks and run.
All at once the alley is empty.
Nothing left but old bricks and graffiti.

As two policemen walk the beat,
I stand in the middle
of this magic trick.

My Focus Fails in Dhyana

Sitting on ground, breathing—

I hear the raspy song of a phoebe
returned to build a nest against my house: *fee bee, fee bee. . .*

Who was I before illness and injury?
Before I was warped by money and work?

Fee bee isn't accurate. A signature buzz distinguishes
phoebe from chickadee to the cadence of *know what*? *Fzz bzz*?

Erratic fanfare of gray and white wings
as this phoebe catches something mid-air.

Who was I before the overwhelming material
of existence? Before parents? Before language?

Gray tail twitches, bewitches. *Fzz bzz*? *Fzz bzz*?

I, too, began with pine needles, sky, and cirrus clouds.
Me as a baby, wanting to be let loose into the woods.

Know what? I'd rather watch this phoebe
weave into her new spring nest a silver strand of tinsel.

Made a Fool

I came to the party wearing a long
white dress and a silk top hat.

I brought my tambourine
and my little terrier, but where was the parade?

Just suits holding wine glasses, swapping
business cards their one dull game.

They snickered at me.
Junior high all over again.

The club leader telling me
to get the ID-10T form to join.

Will I always be sent away
to hunt snipe and fetch glass hammers?

My feet in the sky
as my head hits the ground?

0, dog!
0, dance!

Which Way the Earth?

A toddler, I slapped the globe until it creaked
purely for the spinning.

I flattened tangerine peels into canoes
and learned how segments cloaked a sphere.

In school, I tried to use a mechanical model
of the solar system, but the crank stuck.

I asked my father which way the earth
revolved around the sun: clockwise or counter?

I needed to picture how planets moved.
My father replied: "That depends where you are."

His answer threw me
into a Milky Way of vantage points.   .

If Antarctica tops the planet, all continents point up.
Africa rotates from cashew into comfy chair.

The ice cream cone of South America becomes the wing
of a swan, the bosom of Australia a double-bottomed heart.

The *National Geographic* map cut Asia in half,
positioning where I lived in the center of the wall.

But the world was not flat, and I lost certainty
in what was left and what was right.

Where was I?
Was outer space dark or dazzling?

Pencil Leaf

Leaves drawn with plastic pencils make wallpaper.
Wood pencils lead the lead into the woods—leaves
      become leaves.

One summer, she says she wants to do nothing but draw
      the veins of leaves.
She doesn't. She irons red maple leaves between waxed paper.

Leaf ignores pencil.
Pencil calls leaf Mother.

The Death Jar

My sister's chore was cleaning; mine was killing.
Each summer morning, my mother sent me to her rose garden.
With a flick of my finger, Japanese beetles slipped off pink petals
into a jelly jar half-filled with turpentine.

The beetles, like lacquerwork miniatures, gleamed iridescent
green; hard wings shone copper. Six barbed legs
ended in tiny hooks lifted in curved gestures, holding *kabuki* poses
while they ate. When they flew, they whirred and wobbled.

For sport, I slid a slipknot up a beetle's leg, prodded the beetle to fly,
and delighted in catching the dangling thread, in my power to grab a life
out of mid-air. My sister called me cruel, and I stopped; but why
was it wrong to play with beetles and right to kill them?

My mother cherished her roses so
she couldn't see Japanese beetles had their own elegance,
even though they rendered leaves to skeletons
and carved ugly craters through rose buds. I loved roses, too.

I buried my nose in their pink and golden vortices, and kissed
their petals to feel softness on my lips, to ease the lesson
of summer: that I must destroy beauty to save beauty, while sensing,
in a child's way, that I was more the beetle than the rose.

Blindsided

Riding in my father's car through city lights,
I see one building that's completely dark:

no white windows, no security floods.
Compelling as a ghost, as if three stories

of hand-made brick and narrow windows
time-travelled back before electricity

when textile mills ruled.
My father tells me it's a boarding school

for blind children who don't need lights.
He's cheerful; they're saving money.

I'm upset. I don't think the blind should be
deprived of light because they can't see.

We're going home from the ER.
A doctor from India put five stitches in my head

which I had bashed against a coffee table corner,
and I'm afraid of blind children

dropping nickels into secret piggy banks,
counting steps, tracing fingers against dark walls.

Diary of a Mad Alchemist's Niece

*My grandmother's great uncle, Johann Böttger, was an alchemist
who failed to achieve his goal of turning brass to gold but, under
"custodial" directive by the King of Poland, was the first European
to figure out the formula for porcelain.*

On my eighth birthday, I saw
a complete full-sky double rainbow
and thought it was about me.

All summer I ran
through the sprinkler
for more rainbows on the lawn.

At twenty-four, I crawled
through tunnels from cave to cave,
fearing a burst of bats.

No subterranean rivers. No Styx or Lethe
revealed subconscious secrets. Honestly,
I was relieved to surface and breathe.

After my thirty-third birthday, I climbed
Mt. Fuji. At the base, a black sky deployed meteors.
At the peak, a gray sky dropped hailstones.

No summit sunrise in the fog. No guru.
Only numb tongue, cold bones.
Ice and pumice. Obsidian and obstinance.

Wheels

No need to choose
between helm and roulette.

In time, both will reward
and fail.

As the bicycle you ride
strengthens or injures,

the pinwheel you blow
delights and bores,

the bull's-eye you hit
or miss with your arrows,

luck swings one way
and then the other,

misfortune as likely
as fortune.

That doesn't mean
you'll get both equally.

You can lose and lose and lose,
or always win.

Luck doesn't keep a ledger;
it just swings.

This Glimpse

I never learned how to enter the egg beater
of two ropes swinging Double Dutch.
How to sit wearing a miniskirt.

How to sit next to strangers.
How to include myself when they decide
to go downtown for drinks.

How to drink.
How to talk about myself but not too much.
How to ask for a ride home.

But I know how to walk alone at night.
The snow is invisible except
under a streetlamp—bright tadpoles flying!

Advice

As your father, I would say
learn from your mistakes.

As your mother, I would say
it happens to everyone.

As Adam, I would say
you think too much.

As Eve, I would say
I told you so.

As your friend, I would put my hand
on your shoulder. As your hand,

I would curl beneath your chin
while you thought.

As the floor, I would say
clean up the blood and move on.

As your eyes, I would close.

As the stain on the wall,
I would say I'm a black-winged angel

or an angry badger—and what
does this say about you?

Hand Tools

My father's tools hung on pegboard
in the basement, each in its place:
crosscut saw and coping saw,
plane, pliers, wrenches, hammers,
chisels, rasp, and a harmonica
of translucent yellow screwdrivers
beside the red hand drill. With these,
he put up closet rods, built shelves,
and fixed the house.

He was meticulous.
No job was done
until the tools were put away,
and every speck of sawdust
swept into the dustpan, dumped
in the incinerator.

I was enchanted by his level,
green bubbles trapped in tubes.

When my father was at work,
I sneaked into the basement.
I tapped chalk lines across my legs and arms.
When I traced the coping saw over my palm,
I could perforate my skin without bleeding.
I aimed a drill bit over my heart
and practiced turning the handle.

Devil's Food Cake

After your birthday, you disappeared.
Maybe when you blew out the candles,
the cake inhaled and swallowed
you whole, sucking you through thick
vanilla frosting into the devil's food.

Maybe you are screaming to be let out
and no one can hear you through flour,
sugar, eggs, and sour milk. Maybe
the devil holds your tongue
while you think bloody brown thoughts.

Maybe you are waiting for me to rescue you
with a knife, gently cutting away your prison
crumb by crumb. Maybe you fear growing stale
and getting slopped to the goats.

Maybe you have befriended the devil
and are learning magic tricks inside the cake,
happy with his company and your thoughts.

Maybe you are chewing tunnels, like ants
in their underworld maze. Maybe
you are practicing *qi gong*
surrounded by the perfect porous substance
to make you aware of your every move.

Maybe you will pop out from the cake
and shuck your clothes at a devil convention.

Maybe you are gloating, having shaken me at last.
Maybe you do not want to come back.
Maybe you are standing behind me
watching me cry over a cake baked by the devil.

Too This, Too That

At the party fire pit, he banters with women
he has known since college. Funk from big speakers,
eggplant on the grill, Christmas lights strung
through an avocado tree. He returns a wooden chair
to an ex-girlfriend. He's replaced her broken rung:

no scars, no seams, no mismatched stain.
He's fixing a bicycle rack for another.
All of his exes get along with him and each other,
and years pass. Some recycle as do-overs,
unable to resist a man in love with love.

Before I returned, he assured me he no longer
sought perfection, but I soon became *too this*,
too that again. His twenties, thirties, forties, fifties
look the same on Facebook: a musician on stage,
loneliness hidden inside an upbeat bass.

He scans the crowd for his next ex, unable to choose
between *maybe* and *maybe*. Oh, love could never live
up to the promise of those parties! Barefoot dancers,
silver earrings, goblets of pinot noir, wood smoke
sifted with ocean mist, moon-drenched under live oaks.

Blood Moon

At twilight, my dogs run ahead on slopes of scree
while I walk the train tracks. The ties are spaced to thwart
my gait: too close for one step, too far apart for two.

Between two pines, the full moon reflects the dark side
of the sun. Parallel rails echo moonlight—twin silver serpents.
Hypnotized, I'm pulled into my past.

I am again a virgin hunting love
alone at night, believing in Keats' magic hand of chance
and some unknown good destiny a step or two away.

Again, an insecure flirt, dressed to dance
with men who twirl me once or twice,
but never venture into romance.

A crone with an aura of frizzled silver hair appears,
neck and brow splotched and wrinkled, glad for the silent
awareness of tending two retrievers.

My convoluted path turns into a track so straight and strong
the rails bear the weight of trains. I understand the hazard
of navigating by the moon, meandering like flotsam.

I whisper to my former selves:
use the sextant, do the math,
the stars will steer you safely.

But I can't listen to my self, bedazzled by illusion
that makes this huge white cratered orb
seem close enough to kiss.

Unfinished

He collects pairs of cars—parts from one
to complete the other—that he doesn't repair
as planned. Almost antique Ramblers,
Cutlasses, bulgy-eyed Volvos. He collects hand tools,
discarded books, stray cats, milk bottles, spittoons,
rotary telephones, soprano saxophones.

He rents cheap shacks from oddball landlords
and fills them with plantation decor. A ceramic lamp
disturbed me: a dark-skinned woman kneeling
in a yellow sarong, one hand touching her turban,
the other cupping her naked breast. She reminded him
of Viet Nam: watching bombing from his ship, dropping acid
in Philippine bars. He only falls in love with other men's wives.

But something more than un-winnable women
and un-winnable war wounded his large and lonely heart.
He told me once, in kindergarten, he covered the entire page
with black paint, leaving no room for his name.
He lives in slow motion, as if he had three hundred years
to fill that hole: hours staring into the swimming pool,
his mind spinning with ideas that never get traction,
holding his glass of wine like an offering to someone unseen.

Such Luck

My California single girl bedroom:
cinderblock shelves, futon, paper globe light,
wine bottle candlesticks coated with waxy stalactites.
Lacking men to stay the night, I drank in bed. The more
I drank, the larger my glass grew. I waded surf with cabernet
in hand and yearned for love. Until I sipped and found a fish.

Fish! How did you get in my cup?
    Jumped! Four feet straight up from snapping beaks.
    I could win the Fish Olympics!

What should I do with you, Fish?
    Don't dump me out! Those shags are hungry!

Fish, how do you speak—and why?
    Because you're listening! This is amazing!

Are you real or imaginary?
    Yes!

Do you have some lesson to teach me?
    No!

What kind of fish are you?
    A talking fish! The best kind!

We talked till Fish's gills began to dry.
I walked the length of the longest pier,
far from gulls and cormorants, tossed
and watched him flip four times
before he dove into dark waves.
I tossed my goblet after him,
thinking how lucky I was
to be unlucky in love.

My Mind Wanders in Shavasana

kayaking   my childhood summer lake
          view from the water reveals   screen-doors
small private docks   folding aluminum chairs
          adults in pajamas   drinking coffee   or beer
as sunrise fades   blue imbues a mackerel sky
          less becomes more with the oar my course
                    determined by loons

tailing the winch on my then-boyfriend's sloop
          short handle for fickle winds   the jib responds
like a hooked fish   a moment of tilt and speed
          through the chop   salt lapping stern   toward
a bobbling turtle   trajectory of whale
          double arc of dolphins

rowing synchronized with seven others
          while coxswain commands   muscles pressured
in parallel sweep   our rhythm against the river's
          my back to our goal   measuring progress
                    by furrows of wake

I assume the perspective of a hovering gull
          my strained shoulders   now effortless wings
I look down to see the entire boat as if a leaf
          eight oars symmetrical veins   tipped with white
splash-dots   motion made motionless
          the struggle of the race   gone
why did I fervently want to win?
          the fastest flying   is still

on my mottled blue mat   in a dim room
          hands above my head   thumb touching thumb
one leg straight   one knee bent   I can't tell if I am
          right side up   or upside down

The Bad Lands Spoke

I mean, I *heard* them. Like cicadas and didgeridoo
braiding my brain, masking the car radio. The sound
sifted through layers of ash and sandstone
over old black shale, crescendoed and faded from buttes
and canyons, overlapping, replicating, as if filtered
into my blood pressure.

I couldn't stand it,
couldn't understand it,
didn't want it to stop.

At my first truck stop, off I-90 near Box Elder,
tattooed men in idling rigs eyed my teenage legs.
A big burger filled my stomach, emptied my guts.
A torn towel on a nail was my view from the foul toilet,
but above a stained sink, an open window shone gold.

I still see that yellow sunset fading
over millions of years of sediment,
over thousands of inches of erosion,
an aftermath imbuing the sky with coral & tan
& gray of rattlesnakes that matched the ground.
As grays darkened, moonlight
translated folded rocks into books
I could never read.

No beauty
was more honest
than this stark expanse
below a vast, star-punctured sky
where, by myself, invaded & surrounded
& protected by some inexplicable inner song,
I never felt less alone.

Rubble

Wind wrestles our windows. Something snaps:
instantly, the two of us powerless in the dark.

No internet, no phones. No electricity for the well pump
means no water. Our toilets won't flush.

I picture a tree leaning on power lines;
I once drove under a struck pine with smoking branches—

a foolish risk just to get home faster.
Memories of damage invite us to more destruction.

Flashlights dead from neglect, we do the wrong thing:
stand by the big window to glimpse, in lightning spritzes,

how sturdy oak trees sway, leaves flipped inside-out and silver.
And you, my love, in silhouette assume the shape of your father

who smacked your head until you seized, declared your talents
worthless. Perhaps I mimic my complaining mother?

We stay silent to keep your father from hitting my mother.
Must we be destined to curate our childhood dynamics?

When I light a candle, my mother and your father disappear.
We can hold hands and be afraid.

The dead oak collapses on our storage shed—the house jumps!
Come morning, air rife with deer flies and mosquitoes,

the gentle black snake glides through rubble,
and milkweed blossoms into pink fireworks.

Moving

We confront accumulation. No room
exempt from purge; no cupboard left for later.

The dump pile: broken furniture,
ancient computers, worn tires. The shredder grinds
tax returns from the Paper Age.

But what of our outdated mix tapes, those amateur
epistolaries of our moods? Do we jeopardize
our future if we discard our history? Can we let go

of the frayed comforter without losing comfort?
What will happen to our first leather jackets
we so loved for protecting our jittery egos?

Decisions bludgeon us unconscious.
I wake to a blurry moon framed by an open window,
suddenly aware our attic is full of forgotten boxes.

In pajamas, I lift a corrugated flap and startle
a skeleton. A sepia skull with still-white teeth, tibia, fibula,
a clavicle shaped like a bull's horn, fractured ribs. Who

boxed these bones? The next box holds a ladder
of smirking vertebrae that were once a painful spine.
I tear open box after box and find flat fragile scapulas,

pelvises like steampunk gas masks, finger bones reaching
from mottled clusters of carpus. One skeleton with wings
flies to the rafters, dangling over me, and as I cry out, doomed,

this skeleton assures me everything
will be all right once we move on.

Union Cards on Hallowe'en

Union cards slither between stacks of essays on my floor.
Some are incomplete or lacking names, and from three lists
that should but do not match, some adjuncts won't respond.

Some rage at me, the messenger, who warns
suspended pay is not a trick but labor law.
Cards must be signed before the deadline—Hallowe'en.

I see myself in hero-garb, the champion who fights for wages
of the poorly paid. But those who don't comply, I think, view me
as their antagonist, afraid of those who fire us.

I raked my driveway clean so children wouldn't fall.
Tonight, some children baring bloody fangs came to my door,
helped themselves to candy, ran off littering my lawn.

Now, in my ragged witchy nightgown, after a shot of bourbon,
I listen to Bach's cantata, *Ich habe genug*, followed by Janis Joplin's
Me and Bobby McGee, while yellow leaves and snow saunter

from the cold and clouded sky to fill my gutter,
and slowly build, around my porch light globe,
a larger world.

Aphasia Blues

I called for a pitch
and he heard me call him a bitch
(and he is).

I know this song inside out,
yet the third verse lyrics evaporate
leaving me to scat.

Should I quit my gig at the knife club?
My experienced lungs have power
to hold notes higher

than a diving board, longer than a river.
The music may be better wordless, now
that my mouth spills out wrong words,

my tongue and teeth
more honest than my brain,
my hearing truer than fact.

My fumbler and meddler raised me
to be precise. Though my lips stumble,
my reading of Chinese and Japanese is butter.

This midlife transition symptom is a phase
called Off Asia—and it is much
like riffing off ideograms.

Ki is four strokes that show a pine tree,
sidestepping our bossy temporal lobes.
What is A, anyway? A tent? A ladder?

The bitch gives me an A;
today I climb a ladder leaning on 木 —
today I swing the blues.

The Winter of Our Marriage

For several months, this snow
has held us under siege, indentured servants
of the shovel, supplicants at the altars of power lines.

We drive through gray crystallized mazes,
forced into potholes, blind at every corner.
Our eyes burn from ceaseless white:

walls, windows, ground, and sky. I threaten
to paint each room lime green and you almost agree.
We hunker under the blanket we call Old Sparky,

and our old cat chisels herself between us.
After midnight, a full moon makes the clouded sky
bright as day—and pink?

I wake you; you confirm the sky is pink.
We never figure out the mystery.

The Green Room

The sunrise surfers wake and walk and wait in darkness
through mist or rain, as gray dawn evolves
an edge of yellow, pink, or paler gray.
Each morning, these surfers paddle into cold wet salt
to find the line where weighty water breaks
and wait again for waves—flat or barrel,
smooth or chop.
Regardless of weather, sky, or waves, they practice
balance and strength,
entrance and exit.
The powerful part of the wave is the pocket
ahead of the break.

The word *love*—like *dude*—can mean anything
depending on inflection.
The heart releases trauma when it loves,
when it takes the drop
into the tube and soars
through the green room
on and under the ocean.
The perfect wave does not show up for us;
we show up for it, embracing imperfection,
even when waves draw back and expose the sea bed—
even when they suck the sea bed dry
and strand us in sand and rotting kelp—especially then.
For love is not a gift but a job:
every morning no matter what
into the ocean.

SUCH

Equinox + Duck

This day, when eggs can stand and balance on their own
requires the courage to reconcile contradictions:

dim mornings as the sun shifts south, pulling
warblers in its path, brown weasels' thick fur

growing white, green squash gone gold,
new corn shucked from a withered stalk.

The silver iris re-blooms, its June fragrance
a living ghost.

*

The nun slips off her convent shoes and wades
the brook. Cold water shocks her feet.

A brown mallard dabbles for weeds.
Brood grown and gone, she shakes off

obligation, unwittingly
flinging drops of water on the nun

who watches the duck flap-flap up—up!
and feels her own large creaky wings unfold.

Calligrapher

Animal spirits hover, curious to watch
what I make from their remains: cow skin
parchment, weasel fur brush, goose wing feather,
fish bone ink. So much at stake to mark & mar.

A paradox of exactitude, I must relax
to control the quill or metal nib,
to unify size & slant as I translate
words to shapes, music to curved flags.

Behold my monastery masterpiece!
As grapes into wine went silence
into script, the secret of my fingerprints
ink-stained for all to see.

Go ahead, sing this page!
Veni creator spiritus!
I know you sense it in you
many lifetimes later:

the wildness of ink, its flow & fade,
spread & flake, the magical powers
of sandalwood & cinnabar & clove
& heart strike of vermillion.

I Asked the Alchemist

How do I change white into silver?
He said add gray and adjust the light.

That's how I fell from my ladder
into the ruins of a grotto,
neck and shoulder and elbow burning,
unable to move, wondering
if another silver seeker
would find me as I found—
eye close to ground—
this tiny ladder of wild lilies
making their own white light.

Light Sleeper

The green light from the cable box, winking
like the eye of a nebula, bounces messages off the night sky.

The laptop light shines a dot of orange, like transitive Arcturus,
recharging the battery until its light, too, turns green.

From the turned-off TV, a giant red Betelgeuse shoulders
the arm that pulls Orion's unseen bowstring taut,

mirrored by the red Antares of the phone, the heart
of the scorpion, rivaling the god of war.

The printer beams blue as Sirius, a tiny yet powerful light
erasing all remaining shadows from the room.

This constellation never fades: no darkness arrives to reveal
the abundance of invisible suns our closest sun outshines.

Come morning, the restless sleeper leaves the curtains closed
and opens large screens of light.

Circus Therapy

Before the circus rises on the field
conquering grass with guy wires, stakes, and ropes;
before it breathes through red-striped canvas lungs,
deploying magic cats and elephants
to hypnotize the children, tempting them
to stand between two horses as they run,
or spin on wheels while knife-throwers define
the boundary between bodies and souls,
the fortune teller works the coffee shop.
She writes her orders in symbolic script,
wipes tables, swiping coins and stuffing bits
of whispered gossip in her rolled-up sleeves.
No fortune seekers recognize her when,
with crystal ball, she sells them back their lives.

Blue Inside Green

Playing in the kitchen after dinner with three nesting bowls—
blue inside red, red inside green—the child pours water
back and forth between them, inventing a story
about three trees traveling in a boat through a typhoon.

Though he doesn't know the word *typhoon*, he feels
the violent rocking of three toothpicks stuck in a cork
that seems to drown but rises to the surface of any sized bowl,
green, red, or blue. He's not aware he is training his brain

to associate *green* with *big*, *blue* with *small*,
and himself with traveling trees. He has yet to meet
the green and blue ocean that will become his life's work.

But plenty of time to slop water on his mother's floor
before she carries him to bed, his arms around her neck,
as a coral ribbon of sun presents the sky to the stars.

Green Men Don't Talk

After that dream in which I kill someone
or someone kills me, I start to see

the Green Man: his leafy face,
his clothes of vines and vegetables,

his foliate head carved in an old church door
and in a bookplate, oak leaves sprouting from his ears.

I see him in the supermarket, thumping
watermelons. He sports a mustache of asparagus,

ragged beet green lips, and peas for eyes. I see him
lumber in the woods through shimmering poplar leaves.

At the beach, in a seaweed turban and banana-leaf boardies,
he hangs ten off the nose of a shark. In the restaurant,

he chomps celery stalks, his putrescent jacket covered
with lichen and mushrooms. At the park, an arbor vitae

breaks loose from its hedge and stumbles toward me,
holding a bottle of ale in an outstretched branch.

"Green Man!" I shout. "What do you mean?"

But green men never speak. And so, I drink
with him on a splintered bench, and fall asleep.

The Genius

She's busy staring at a ragged alder leaf
backlit by setting sun: its complex
simplicity, fractals repeated in varying scale.

The word *scale* invites fish and symphonies.
She hears salmon muscling upstream and tastes
the cayenne of the xylophone
amid the low vibration of cello and bass.

She appears to be doing nothing, but only a brain
at rest allows patterns to reveal themselves,
the interface of world and mind its own sublimity.

On the brink of unlocking music and waves,
she is interrupted by people who want to pay her
to achieve something. Oh, the time
they force her to waste saying *no, no, no.*

Needle

A splinter of bone makes a needle
that can prod a splinter out of flesh.

A needle can shrink a swollen knee
or swell a basketball.

A needle in the lobe pierces your ear with gold.
A needle through your ear drum silences the world.

Lovers needle each other,
taking stitches in the heart.

A needle plunges poison in your veins
or pulls out blood to reveal your cure.

Two needles fashion a sweater to warm your chest.
Two needles hold thick hair to cool your neck.

Pine needles live three years.
Their fragrance heals your lungs.

Several needles, well-placed, mend a tendon.
Drinking one needle can kill you.

A needle can drag a dead singer back to life
or scratch her vocal cords.

A red needle signals you are running out of gas.
A quivering needle aligns with the North Star.

The Perfectionist's Wife

To demonstrate the floor was clean enough
to eat on, he dumped his bowl of oatmeal
onto ceramic, knelt beside the buttery
mess, and lowered his head to feed.

He hadn't imagined this would be hard.
Pain lodged in his elbows and knees,
his nose in the way, his teeth
scraping tile, lip muscles weak

from using forks and spoons. Worse,
his discerning tongue found a cat hair
after he'd scrubbed the floor to set an example
for his lazy wife. Rump in the air,

he turned into a donkey, determined to win
the battle of cleanliness versus sloth.
Meanwhile, his wife, in bed, still fed the baby,
her nipple plugging his toothless mouth

as he slugged warm milk. She heard
her husband bray and saw their cow, the one
that had begun to grow wings, gauge the distance
between the pasture and the morning crescent moon.

Fist of the Phoenix

In the presence of fortune-tellers, I fold
my fingers into fists to keep secret
my lines // my life, my love, my work

I'm such a hypocrite // I learned
Chinese astrology, my daily to-do
based on twelve animals, five elements

I was born a chicken drawn to flame
a golden dragon almost killed me
wood horse brought a scrap of fame

but superstition isn't fate // the future
continues not to exist // I want my hands
to cradle as much as they can handle

the dough I knead to grow on its own //
rising each night while I sleep // my fingers
instinctively finding their *ur*-fists

Diabolus Ex Machina

God waits in the theater rafters
in white robes, with straps
that wrap his torso to a crane's hook
that will lower him onto the stage
at the cue of a trumpet. His drop-in speech
is the quick save for his writer's poor plot,
for only a god can make
the ludicrous convincing.

The devil lounges below the floorboards,
listening to footsteps crisscross above his head.
He knows each move and line: the understudy
for every actor. He waits by the trap door
to catch the one who falls into his lap, to pamper
him with wealth and petty power, ply him
with cognac, and then assume his role on stage.

The Man Who Is Never Wrong

He shreds paper into a top hat,
waves his wand, and pulls out a white rabbit,

assured of his talent in misdirection. He, too,
watches his hand with the wand, ignoring

his hand in the hat. A magician is never wrong.
He adroitly shifts the world from round to flat,

several lies ahead of fact-checkers,
truth-seekers, and women who fall in love
with him by proxy for the idea that change is easy.

The man who is never wrong has no qualms
about altering past or predicting future.
He lives for an audience that is never right,

that confirms his power by believing the wand,
believing rabbits materialize from hats

to vanish after the show
instead of trundling into cages
to eat pellets in a plastic dish.

Someday, I'll sneak backstage and steal the rabbit.
We'll find a field of alfalfa and live by principles

of matter and uncertainty, on a watery globe
that circles a fiery sun.

Chess Therapy

I play both sides of the chess board
alternating white and black. I fight and switch

becoming my own worst enemy
and then the enemy of my enemy

I must watch closer. I'm not sure who wins
when I lose, this process my triumph.

One-step, two-step pawns set up challenges
until a cornered king lies down.

When the game ends, the journey begins.
Alone, without the comfort of his square,

the crownless king must find the man within,
give up e1/e2 to feel the fibers of the rug,

to learn its pattern where his shadow falls,
and dream his way beyond the castle walls.

Sixth Century Particle Theory

Not only every human but every leopard
had a soul, and every antelope.
The cobra had a soul, and its venom,
and every sloughed skin.

The parrot had a soul, and its eggs
and broken shells had souls,
and a soul for the speck of pinfeather
stuck in dried albumen, and for the nest.

Palm trees had souls,
and souls for roots and fallen coconuts,
and dead fronds knocked down
were alive with souls, on sand
that gleamed with a soul for every grain,
and a separate soul for each pebble, each shell.

A droplet of cold rain had a soul,
and each flame of fire and each ash,
and the monsoon wind
blowing through centuries
into electrons and neutrinos humming
with innumerable splintering souls.

His Wheat Dream

He wants a patch of wheat
instead of a bluegrass lawn.
Not for grain or profit,
but to see the shape of the wind
as it pushes through sunny tassels,
blowing gold into silver.

Pica Pica

"We did not find evidence of an unconditional attraction to shiny objects in magpies. Instead, all objects prompted responses indicating neophobia—fear of new things—in the birds."
                    —Dr. Toni Shephard, August 2014.

O, raucous Magpie, smart and flashy,
maligned for picking up and hiding what scares you!

I, too, am cast as a bad omen. Do they call us thieves
because we rob them of superstitions?

One for sorrow	You grieve.
Two for mirth	You mate for life.
Three for a wedding	You eat cake.
Four for a death	You grieve. You feed.
Five for silver	You fear.
Six for gold	You fear.
Seven for a secret	You recognize yourself in a mirror.
Eight for heaven	You sing *pure-pure.*
Nine for hell	You yell *wock-a-wock.*
Ten for the devil's own self	You are blamed.

We know what we look like and who we are.
We know silver and gold are up to no good.

We seek warm cherries at the top of the tree.

Bad Luck

Like a goldfinch at a feeder
fending off other birds,

the bent-back woman
in a stained yellow muumuu

scrapes her lottery ticket
in front of its vending machine,

preventing interlopers
from scoring the jackpot

she thinks she will earn
by using up the bad luck

one ticket at a time.

Leaving the City Behind

The first city you picture when someone says *city*
is your love city, the one you learned by foot,
whose concrete abraded the soles of your shoes,

whose subway map still appears in your PET scan,
whose towers of glass skies and doorways of urine
revealed how rich rich people really are, how poor the poor.

You rented a studio: tiny floor, tall walls, curved window,
five locks on the door. You answered
phones, made copies, added numbers, poured coffee.

This city trained you to sense buses coming,
distinguish Bhutanese and Tagalog, to know
the taste of rabbit from goat.

In the daily treasure hunt of your love city,
you found an all-poetry bookstore with wing chairs
from a thrift store next to a neon stripper bar.

Gradually, you discovered you fell in love
with all your lovers because they were part of the city.
They flattened and shrank in the nearest field.

Leaving the city is not the same
as leaving the city behind.
You leave the city by car or ferry or phone.

You leave behind what has challenged and changed you
into someone able, at last, to follow a black swan
without fear—to become who you are outside of the city.

The Menu at the Bridge

He had been warned, but snow-blind, feverish
from hours of hiking, lost in blizzard winds,
his toes and fingers paralyzed, his cap
frozen into the nest of icicles
that once had been his hair, he found the inn.
No words or stories mattered, only life;
and nothing less than God's breath on his neck
could stop his feet from climbing up the steps
as clumps of ice fell through the metal grate
and dropped into deep whiteness far below.
His boots put up a fight. A boy in green
appeared, and pulled them off, then led him to
a raw plank table near a golden fire
taller than a man, hotter than a forge.

*

As movement melted back into his hands,
and echoes of the wind lodged in his ears
subsided, he began to drink. Strong tea
with brandy opened his cold throat and heart.
He ate potatoes drenched in cheese, coarse bread,
a salty chicken soup, and apple pie.
After the meal, the green boy handed him
a menu with four choices: A, B, C,
or D. "Is this a game?" he asked. "A joke?"
The green boy shook his head and without words
informed him that he must decide before
he crossed the bridge. "What bridge is this?"
The boy did not reply. The hiker slept
on a bunk bed among three empty beds.

*

That night, he had no dreams he could recall,
yet something fearful woke him before dawn.
A gibbous moon was shining on the snow.
He saw the inn clung to a wall of cliff,
from which a footbridge made of rope spanned
a chasm across a mighty frozen flume
the height of five cathedrals. On the bridge,
three pale men dressed in bones trudged toward him.
They carried axes with a letter marked
on each: A, B, and C. At once, before
they claimed their bunks, before his instinct waned,
the hiker rushed to tell the green-spined boy:
"My choice is D!" The boy led him outside
and deftly pushed him off the precipice.

Jack

I have become the smaller flag on a ship,
the shorter rafters of a roof, a knave
in a pack of cards. I wear a skimpy coat,
tall leather boot, and leather drinking flask.
I am captured in a child's game
and hit when grown men gamble.
I am what they call a tame ape.

I was a common man
whose job was to lift weight.
Mechanical devices that replaced
my muscles took my job and pay
and more—they took my human name.
And I, who used to pull
my master's boots, hoist meat
and turn the spit, work the roller
and the winch, climb the steeple,
strike the bell, and connect lines
in telephone exchange, am a daw,
the tiniest of crows, gathering
loose sticks to nest in castle ruins.

The solace of six centuries—and still—
is once, on a high and windy hill,
beside a well that was clear and full,
I kissed a girl named Gylle.

Stella at Sunrise

Ninety and naked, she grabs
two pitchers of water
from the assistant's unguarded cart
and sneaks outside.

The pitchers weigh on her frail arms,
slow her aching hips as she puts
one bare foot after another
on damp lawn.

Reaching the marsh, she sits
on a splintered bench, gathering strength
to finish her mission: to pour water
on the mangrove

where she believes she found
a roseate spoonbill's nest,
and to water the marsh itself,
to make its waning level rise.

She has no doubt
she will meet the spoonbill
soon. Eyes shut,
she sees pink feathers.

Ezekiel Remembers the Sky

I remember the silence of the sky
when people looked up at the buzz
of a low-flying four-seater airplane.

Everyone lived in four dimensions,
drove four wheels,
had four faces.

My job-face was an ox.
I plowed through the day, curbing
my urge to run to the lake.

My love-face was a lion,
muscular and fierce, hard hunger
swelling below my ribs.

My self-face was only part human.
Sometimes I was a humble witch,
sometimes a black-winged angel.

My spirit-face confronted me beak-first:
a brown-eyed, dirt-feathered eagle.
I still dream in bird's-eye view.

As the sky grew louder, our faces faded.
We became one-faced and two-mouthed,
filling the air with fumes and chatter.

I remember the sky, almost
quiet enough to hear clouds breathe . . .
shattered by church bells.

After the Circus Leaves

A scarecrow jumps down from his pole
to gather, in his clumsy straw-filled sleeves,
the litter—ticket stubs, cigarette butts, sequins,
paper cotton candy cones, flex straws, coins,
ripped mustard packets, tiny plastic shards—
cleaning his field.

A clown's discarded red ball nose—
his prize find!—he puts on his burlap face
and walks with a bit of samba in his step
back to his post, where he gazes skyward
and pretends to juggle
three circling crows.

Candle Ritual

At dusk, we bring wine and wood to a small caldera
in a large grass field where we sit with our own fire
to watch candles on the hillside horizon tremble into flame.

A candle for the horse who carries us
and one for the cow whose milk sustains us.

A candle for faceless masses who fear and pray
and one for the woman who rides with her spear held high.

A candle for the grave of the silver-haired grandmother
and one for the cradle of the golden-haired baby boy.

A candle for the skull that protects the brain
and one for the hand that reaches for a knife.

A candle for the white cobra who kills
and one for the black snake who heals.

The hills, speckled with quivering candles,
resemble a starlit sky, while the sky's last light
mimics the subtle purple of distant mountains.

Throw the wine on the ashes!
What surrounds us is our celebration.

Acknowledgements

I'm happy to thank the editors who first published these poems, some in earlier versions:

Allegro (UK): Made a Fool
Anima (UK): Chess Therapy
Bamboo Ridge: The Death Jar; Fist of the Phoenix; Wheels
Bracken: I Asked the Alchemist
Crannóg (Ireland): Candle Ritual; Now's the Time; Pica Pica
Don't Talk to Me About Love: Too This, Too That
Dreams & Nightmares: The Menu at the Bridge
Gargoyle: Advice; Aphasia Blues; The Man Who Is Never Wrong
—hence, tirade: Union Cards on Hallowe'en
Hermes Poetry Journal (UK): Diary of a Mad Alchemist's Niece
Hermeneutic Chaos Literary Journal: Hand Tools
Intima: A Journal of Narrative Medicine: Needle
Marathon Literary Review: Which Way the Earth?
Mithila Review (India): The Genius
Modern Poetry Quarterly Review: Diabolus Ex Machina
New Welsh Reader (UK): The Perfectionist's Wife
Noble / Gas Qtrly: Stella at Sunrise
PANK: Devil's Food Cake
The Pedestal Magazine: Moving; Such Luck; Unfinished
Poetry Magazine: Jack
Polu Texni: Blood Moon
The Rialto (UK): Sixth Century Particle Theory
Rust + Moth: Blindsided
Silver Blade: After the Circus Leaves; Ezekiel Remembers the Sky; Equinox + Duck
Snapdragon: A Journal of Art & Healing: Blue Inside Green
So to Speak: Circus Therapy
Star*Line: Green Men Don't Talk
SWWIM: The Winter of Our Marriage
Tar River Poetry: Rubble
The Lake: The Light Sleeper
Turtle Island Quarterly: The Bad Lands Spoke; Calligrapher; The Green Room; Leaving the City Behind; Pencil Leaf
unstamatic: His Wheat Dream

I'm also happy to acknowledge the publishers of these reprints:

Writing in a Woman's Voice: The Genius
from the chapbook *Bicycle Lotus* (Left Fork): My Focus
   Fails in Dhyana
from the chapbook *Scavenger Hunt* (dancing girl press):
   Devil's Food Cake
from *The 2019 Poetry Nook Anthology* (White Plum
   Press): Aphasia Blues; Candle Ritual; Chess Therapy;
   Ezekiel Remembers the Sky; Hand Tools; I Asked the
   Alchemist; Leaving the City Behind; Needle; Sixth
   Century Particle Theory

I thank all my fellow writers and readers who have aided my efforts in so many ways—for conversations about poetry and life, for comments about my poems, for support and encouragement, and for the stimulation of what they read and write.

I could not ask for better friends than Eric Paul Shaffer whose insights, clarity, and ability to simultaneously laugh and shout over the phone continue to inspire, and Michael Spring whose steadfast faith in the value of my poetry saw me through the entire process of drafting, revising, and publishing this collection. Such Luck indeed!

I am grateful for the luck that led me to David, who has put up with me for sixteen years: so far so good.

About the Author

Sara Backer has lived in Costa Rica, Japan, and both coasts of the United States. She earned an M.A. in English from the University of California at Davis and an M.F.A. in Poetry from Vermont College of Fine Arts. She has published a novel, *American Fuji* (Penguin Putnam), and two poetry chapbooks: *Bicycle Lotus* (Left Fork) which won the *Turtle Island Poetry Award*, and *Scavenger Hunt* (dancing girl press). Her writing has been honored with fellowships from the Djerassi and Norton Island artist residency programs. She currently lives in the woods of the Merrimack River watershed, teaches at UMass Lowell, and leads reading groups at a men's prison. Her website is sarabacker.com. *Such Luck* is her first book of poetry.

CPSIA information can be obtained
at www.ICGtesting.com
Printed in the USA
BVHW071446071019
560429BV00009B/810/P